HOW TO MEDITATE ON GOD'S WORD

Grow in love, prayer, worship and intimacy with God through intentional Biblical Meditation

Samuel O. Wilson

How to meditate on God's word

Grow in love, prayer, worship and intimacy with God through intentional Biblical Meditation

Samuel O. Wilson

Copyright © April 2017

Visit our website:
www.engraftify.com

Contents

INTRODUCTION

Moses had done his best. He had fought a good fight and kept the faith. The time was up for Moses, and he had to bow out. The mantle of authority was transferred to someone else. The man was Joshua. God had chosen Joshua to lead the children of Israel to the Promised Land. Joshua was ready but would have to go by instructions else he fails. God had given some instructions to Joshua, but one stood out which was very critical to his success or failure to carry out the assignment. Even till this day, that instruction is still relevant if we will have to succeed or fail in our lives.

As Christians, it doesn't matter what we go through in life but how we can apply God's Word to our situation and have Him manifest in it. God's Word is a tool for victory. You can't triumph in your challenges, trials or temptation with weapons of men but with that of the Spirit which is the Word of God. Again, God's Word can make you succeed significantly beyond material riches. Biblical meditation remains the ultimate formula for getting God's Word manifest in our lives.

God said to Joshua, "This book of the law shall not depart out of thy mouth; but thou shalt meditate therein day and night, that thou mayest observe to do according to all that is written therein: for then thou shalt make thy way prosperous, and then thou shalt have good success." –Joshua 1:8. If Joshua would have to succeed taking the children of Israel to the Promised Land, then he would have to heed to that instruction. That was the most important thing he needed to do in the midst of other things.

Did Joshua succeed with this instruction? If yes, then you also can succeed greatly with everything that you have to do even where others failed or in your challenges by doing what Joshua did—meditating on the Word of God. It's easy to apply God's Word in your trials and temptation and get a result. It has nothing to do with the magnitude of your problems before you. Those problems are there so that you can exercise the Word on them. To shy away from your problems is to deny the manifestation of the Word; to shy away from utilizing the power of the Word to make yourself prosperous is to accept struggles and live with your challenges like others in the world. Remember, many are in tears even with their material riches. When God said, "…for then thou shalt make thy way prosperous, and then thou shalt have good success," this goes beyond material blessings.

In simple terms, God said to Joshua:

1. You must look into the book of the law.

2. You must read it.

3. You must keep the laws in your heart.

4. You must keep declaring them.

Doing these things would ultimately mean doing what the law says, and these are the things Joshua did, and the man was prosperous both physically and spiritually. He held on to the laws of God and succeeded with it. Even today, there are no shortcuts to walking around succeeding in your spiritual life and extending to your physical life. If you cannot succeed in your spiritual life, you cannot succeed in your physical life because the spiritual controls the physical. This is why you need the Word of God. This is why you must meditate on it. As Joshua did, you must take this one instruction seriously as a child of God if you want to experience true success in your life and win life battles.

The book of the law today is the Word of God in our hands—the Holy Bible. You must read it, meditate on it and declare it if you desire true success as Joshua did. We will look further into these steps in the course of this book. Meditation on the Word of God helps us to understand God and what He wants from us. It helps us to pay attention to the Word and see the person of the Word. The Word is a person; you must know the Word and the Word must know you before the Word can become one with you. This can only be achieved through effective meditation on God's Word. This is the only way you can experience consistent breakthrough and victory in your life and strengthen your relationship with God.

The Bible isn't like any other book. You can't read it as though you were reading a history book or some novels. It won't produce any result for you that way. You must invite the Holy Spirit to guide you, read and meditate on the Word to come alive in you and become a tool in your hands.

Sadly, meditation isn't easy as it sounds. You may not get the right result from it if you do it wrong. However, as Christians, our lives depend on what we can make out of God's Word and hence, we don't have a choice that to learn how to meditate on the Word effectively. The world would continue to be in the fast lane with happenings that challenges our focus on the Word. But that's Satan strategy to get our attention divided, but we must resist him and maintain our focus on what the Word says rather than what happens around us.

We must refuse to be carried away by breaking news, political news, social media, domestic affairs, propaganda, violence, fears, etc. These things would always be there and even growing in proportion to take our focus away from the Word. When we can't concentrate and meditate on the Word to produce in us what it talks about, the Word becomes ineffective, and we become like religious people tossed to and fro by every wind of doctrine. The Word gives us strength, peace, hope, encouragement, answer to our troubles and everything we can ever think of or desire in our lives. We can't afford to live without meditating on the Word.

In a nutshell, this book contains guidelines to help you meditate effectively on the Word of God and have an encounter with the person of the Word which is Jesus Christ. I am confident that this book would positively impact your relationship and faith in God.

Chapter 1

UNDERSTANDING BIBLICAL MEDITATION

What comes to the mind of many people when meditation is mentioned is an idea of creating some spiritual quietness within the mind through mystical or existentialistic efforts. However, the meditation we are talking about here is entirely different from that, and we won't be looking into detail of the new age meditation in this book. As Christians, our form of meditation is referred to as Christian or Biblical meditation.

Biblical meditation supersedes every other form of meditation as everything we will ever need in life as humans can only be found in the Word of God and not in anything else. The Christian meditation comes from the old Hebrew word: "hagah" which means "to utter," "to devise," "to muse," or "to mutter." Utter means to speak; while muse means "to consider thoughtfully and thoroughly." These rudiments form the basis of our meditation. From here we can define **Christian meditation as an act of uttering the scripture with our mouths, considering it thoughtfully and thoroughly; talking and**

turning it over and over again in our hearts to make it a part of us to declare same in faith.

The Word of God is the object of our meditation. We don't meditate on anything or try to achieve quietness or empty our minds as others do in the new age meditation, we meditate on the Word. We were made of the Word, and we must always talk the Word—loudly or quietly in our hearts.

You can never sit completely quiet. Life is a talking one because we were made of the Word. It is through what goes on in our hearts that we voice what we have to say from there. What we all do is always as a result of the thoughts we processed in our minds. This is why God wants to take over our hearts through meditation on the Word—our life manual. Once God can take over our hearts, we begin to act according to His will for our lives and not according to our selfish minds because we are selfish.

We were born only with human knowledge and her ways of doing things and until we grow up and feed our spirits with God's Word, we will remain unknowledgeable in the ways of God and continuously limited in the affairs of life. Meditation in the Word purges the ways of the world from us and infuses in us the ways of God. We begin to talk and act with God through meditation. Biblical meditation is a deliberate effort to become aware of and ponder on the revelations of

God. The Word of God cannot become a revelation to you because you merely read it. You must understand and own it before you can use it to create changes.

The Psalmist wrote, *"O how I love thy law! It is my meditation all the day. Thou through thy commandments hast made me wiser than mine enemies: for they are ever with me."* – Psalm 119:97-98. Meditation isn't a contemporary subject but a powerful tool to know and obey the Word of God. It has always been there, but only a few take advantage of knowing God through meditation. The above is just a tip of the iceberg that meditation would do for you. If you love the Word of God, meditate on it all day long. Don't allow any wrong thoughts to come into your mind; fill it with the laws of the Lord. This is the way to go as a child of God. Take it personally; choose to grow in the knowledge and understanding of the scripture. The Word of God would make you clean (*see* John 15:3) and do what it talks about when you give your body, soul, and spirit to it. Delight in the law of the Lord; meditate on it day and night (*see* Psalm 1:2).

Biblical meditation is seeking God's face through His Word. God wants us to tune our thoughts to be in line with His views so that our actions, as a result, can also be in line with His Word and that is true Christian relationship with God. God said in Isaiah 55:7-8, *"Let the wicked forsake his way, and the unrighteous man his thoughts; let him return to the Lord, and He will have mercy on him; and to our God, for He will abundantly pardon. 'For my thoughts are not your thoughts, nor are your ways My ways,' says the Lord."* Most of the challenges and conflicts in our lives today are as a result of our thoughts and myths that have formed our beliefs. Through meditation, we are purged of these wrong thoughts and erroneous beliefs and have the true Word of God takes abode in us and control our thoughts and actions.

Finally, Romans 12:2 crowns it all: *"Be not conformed to this world; <u>but be ye transformed by the renewing of your mind</u>, that ye may prove what is that good, and acceptable, and perfect will of God."* A true transformation of the mind can only happen through meditation on the Word of God.

CHAPTER 2

10 BENEFITS OF
BIBLICAL MEDITATION

We can only be true Christians through meditation and not by our self-will or effort. We can never achieve living true to our Christian cause by our personal efforts. It can only happen through the power of God which is only available in His Word and His Word can only become an integral part of us through meditation.

Jesus said in John 15:7-8,*"If you abide in Me, and My words abide in you, you will ask what you desire, and it shall be done for you. By this My Father is glorified, that you bear much fruit; so you will be My disciples."* This Scripture alludes to what we read in Joshua 1:8 when God said to the man that if he meditates and does what the law says, he will become prosperous and have good success. We can begin to see and be convinced about the importance of meditation already.

We cannot on our own do anything good except we give up our weakness to God and take up His nature through His living Word. As the Word comes to live in us, it cleans us and help us reason and act like God concerning a matter. If God does not act through us, we will continue to reason and work from our human senses which at best are riddled with errors and can't stand the test of time.

Other benefits of meditation include;

Meditation builds faith in us

This is the most important aspect of meditation. As you meditate on God's Word, boldness replaces your fears because you have discovered a way out of your challenges. All your fears vanish and even if a gun is pointed at you, you'll simply know that the Word of God can travel faster than a bullet even without saying it verbally.

What creates fears in us is our ignorance of how we can manage situations in our lives. But with meditation and having the Word alive in you, you take charge of things knowing that God is with you. The more we take up God's Word and make it active in us, the more our faiths spontaneously grow.

Meditation in the Word keeps us close to God

This sounds straight. God is the object of the Word, and a visit to the Word is a visit with God. Once you visit God through His Word, you can choose to stay with Him by keeping the Word in your heart and turning it over and over again, warming your heart with it and experiencing impartation from the Word.

Through meditation, we truly know that we know

There are levels of knowledge. At some levels, you can easily get convinced to change your mind about what you know but when you begin to meditate on God's Word, you become confident about what you know and believe in your heart, and no one can convince you otherwise. You truly know that you know.

Meditation on the Word makes us to be grounded in the Word and hold on firmly to it. From here, the only thing happening next is to be changed by the Word in us positively.

Meditation helps us to put Satan where he belongs

Satan belongs under our feet, but without personalizing the Word of God through meditation, he will still be able to manipulate your mind. God's Word is the antidote to keep Satan and his demons off our lives. They come throwing wrong thoughts into our minds so that we can yield to those thoughts and fall off the radar of God. But with God's Word running through us, we can always declare them to the devil, and he will flee.

The Word says, "Therefore, submit to God. Resist the devil, and he will flee from you" (*see* James 4:7). Sadly, you can't resist the devil just as it sounds in the scripture. You can only resist him through the engrafted Word living in you.

Meditation sets and keeps us on God's plan and purpose

Our human nature would always want to think and act like a human it is; it always look for ways of fulfilling the desires of the flesh, but with God's Word living in us, our human nature and our thinking is suppressed, allowing the Word to define a purpose for our lives. Then we begin to live without struggles but according to God's plan laid out for us in His Word (*see* Joshua 1:7; Psalm 119:15).

It helps us to become stable in the ways of God

It's a terrible life to live as a babe in Christ. Babes in Christ are like little children who know nothing. They can easily be convinced to believe or do otherwise. God's Word stuck in our hearts help us to be stable and not carried away by every wind of doctrine. There are many Christians who are not stable in their ways; they are still babes in Christ.

Through meditation, we become captured by the Holy Spirit

The Holy Spirit acts in us through our conscience. Some people ask, "How can I hear God talk to me?" It's simple: listen to your conscience. Your conscience can easily tell you if your actions are good or bad. Your heart is the seat of your conscience. As you meditate and teach your conscience the ways of God, it becomes captured by the Holy Spirit and ruled by thoughts from God.

We increase in knowledge, wisdom, and understanding through meditation

God's Word is an embodiment of wisdom. Wisdom does not come through the reading of college materials or any book; wisdom comes from God alone, and wisdom is the principal thing.

The Word of God is God on the pages of a book called the Holy Bible, and until you begin to meditate on it and declare same in faith, it will not make sense to you. While studying the Bible, you don't only increase in knowledge and understanding of the scripture or how things indeed work; you also increase in wisdom. Every other school would have you grow in knowledge and understanding but the college of biblical meditation goes beyond that, it deals with the infallible knowledge of the Word, wisdom and higher understanding both in the things of God and how things work in the world. The deeper you go in meditation, the brighter the eyes of your spirit.

Meditation helps us speak God's Word in our challenges and temptation

God's Word living in us is more than silver and gold. Our true Christian nature is revealed during times of trials and temptation. Our challenges amplify our weaknesses. It reveals to the world what we truly are and not what we claim to be in the absence of problems.

After Jesus fasted for forty days and forty nights, He was hungry. His challenge at the time was hunger, and that was the exact time the devil showed up to tempt Him. But He proved to be the Son of God because of the Word of God in Him and didn't fall for the tricks of the devil. He released the right words that were in Him, and that settled the devil, and he left. You can only overcome your challenges, trials, and temptation with the Word of God in you. When faced with a challenge, you can simply pull out what's inside of you to come out of it. No magic else you get into deeper trouble.

Meditation creates in us a mentality

As we meditate on the scripture and declare those things we take into our hearts in faith, our old thoughts, myths and beliefs are replaced with the true Word of God, and we seize to think and talk like others in the world. This body of new thoughts that ultimately affects our actions gives us a mentality, and we walk not after the flesh anymore but after the Spirit.

In summary, meditation is the only way out for any Christian who wants to maintain a cordial relationship with God and walk in the Spirit. We can't afford to leave our minds to feed on anything. We are a vessel if God cannot occupy us, Satan will. Choose this day who you want to influence your thoughts and actions.

CHAPTER 3

8 STEPS TO EFFECTIVE MEDITATION

You don't simply jump on the Scripture and say you want to meditate on it. You must have a plan in line with your Bible study and also understand the steps to a compelling meditation on God's Word. Meditation is not necessarily a prayer but can lead to it. There are two different things. In the former, God speaks to us through His

Word while in the later; we talk to God in reference to His Word. **Meditation is to take the Word of God, understand and ponder over it in your hearts again and again until you get to the point that you become fully persuaded with the idea of the Word and can then begin to declare same Words over your situations, life and everything that concerns you.**

You meditate to understand, attain persuasion and also speak with faith in your heart concerning what the Word talks about. You don't meditate only to know or understand the Scriptures. This chapter sums up the steps needed for effective meditation.

1. Clear your heart

Our heart is the communication point between the Holy Spirit and us. Real meditation is a spiritual exercise, and the Holy Spirit must be fully part of it. He must be there to help and confirm the words you utter in your heart, and hence, you must prepare your heart to make it comfortable for the Holy Spirit and for the task at hand to be effective. To prepare your heart, clear it from all forms of doubts, grudges, bitterness, offenses, resentment, sadness, etc. You must be free in your spirit. Forgive anyone who has offended you in the past else your effort at meditating on the Scripture would be a total waste. Your heart [or spirit] must be at its best state before meditation, and if you can't get your spirit to be at its best, it's okay to suspend the exercise.

2. Invite the Holy Spirit

The Holy Spirit connects us to the Father. He bears witness in us that we are children of God. In every spiritual exercise, you must invite the Holy Spirit to help and direct. Hence, go ahead and pray the Holy Spirit to guide you and help make your effort to know God more and make your meditation a fruitful one.

3. You must focus your heart on what you do

Remember, the devil is not happy with what you are about to do, and as such he will try to distract you, but you must fix your eyes and heart on the Word of God. Psalm 119:5 admonish us to set our sights on the ways of God. Consciously create time for this; shun other pursuits and refuse to be distracted. When you focus your mind during meditation, understanding becomes easy. If possible, move away from your house to some quiet place surrounded by greens of nature where you can feel the beauty of nature. Such is a perfect environment to raise your spirit and connect with the Holy Spirit. Drop all devices containing electronic Bible and use the Book.

4. Seek to understand every word

When your focus is right, understanding becomes a walkthrough. If possible, have other Bible translations or a Bible dictionary around you to help simplify the verses. Pray as the Psalmist did to God in Psalm 119:27 saying, *"Make me understand the way of your precepts, and I will meditate on your wondrous work."* Reflect on the verses; take out what you need to know or what it says about God. How do the verses apply to you? You must understand what God is telling you through His Word. For example, the Bible says in Philippians 3:13, *"Brethren, I count* *not myself to have apprehended: <u>but this one</u>* *<u>thing I do, forgetting those things which are</u>* *<u>behind and reaching forth unto those things</u>* *<u>which are before</u>.*" If I were to meditate on this Scripture, I would make the following deductions:

(a) What is the Scripture saying here? The Scripture here is talking about an unfavorable past that must be put behind. This is the main focus of this verse.

(b) What do I need to know? I need to know that my unfavorable past, if not left in the past where it belongs, can hurt my future.

(c) What is God telling me? God is telling me to put all my unfavorable past behind and look forward to what lies ahead in Him.

(d) How do I apply the Scripture to my life? Examples; "I must forgive and forget about my partner that promised me marriage and after that disappointed. I must put behind the course I studied so hard for but failed the exam. I must forgive my Dad that vowed never to support my education because I did something wrong. I must put behind the insult I got from my Boss yesterday… and so much more."

Finally, I must keep this Scripture in my heart and remind myself at all times and also preach it to others who may also be struggling with their lives because of their negative past. Teaching others what we learnt help us to get soaked with that thing and never forget them. If what you have learnt from the Word is good, tell it to others let it also influence their thoughts as it has done to you.

5. You must think over and over again what you understand

This step would help you to remember what you read and have it settled in you. Once you have the initial understanding of a Bible passage, you must think over and over and over on it. This is the actual meditation. The more you think about what you have read, the more it sinks in you; the more it becomes a part of you.

The Word of God must form an integral part of you, mixing with your blood and running in you just like the blood does. From here, you become persuaded and simply know that you truly know. If you truly know, nothing can take it away from you.

6. You must remember your meditations

You don't meditate for the sake of it but to use it to cause changes. Again, meditation isn't just for the 'now' but to use the things you have meditated upon as a tool to change circumstances when necessary. We don't go to church to make God happy; we go so that we can pick up the things we learn from there and apply it to our lives and see our lives change. The battle is not in the church but outside of the church.

The action of meditation is not the real work but to remember the things you picked up from the Word of God and declare those things in faith when circumstances arise. As you continue reading this book, you'll learn how to memorize the Bible passages. Once you get it right with step 5 above, you will always remember your meditations and apply it to your life for success.

7. Worship is a part of meditation

If the steps stated above go as it should, worship becomes inevitable. When we take the Word into our heart and see the excellent and beauty of the Word, we are moved to worship. Go ahead and worship Him in the beauty of His Holiness; worship Him for making His Word true in your life. Worship Him for giving you faith to believe in His Word and helping you to keep the Word in your heart as a light to your path. Worship Him because in His Word is true success and victory in times of challenges, trials, and temptations.

8. Apply your meditations to your life

Remember our opening Scripture, Joshua 1:8, *"…that thou mayest observe to do according to all that is written…"* This is the ultimate aim of meditation—to use our meditations to change our thoughts or renew our minds to obey God's command without struggles and walk worthy of emulation in our calling to the place of Christ. Meditate to obey and apply God's Word to your life.

Finally, getting it right from step 1−8 is not an easy task because the devil knows what you stand to become if you do all of these things as stated. He will distract you and make you feel your meditations are in vain but don't give up. Remember, there is no true or good success without God. Ask

Him to help you; fix your eyes on Christ alone with a sincere heart to live worthy of Him. Take the development of your spiritual life a personal affair.

Chapter 4

MEMORIZATION AND MEDITATION

Depending on your perspective, Scripture memorization can be hard and easy. It can be hard for you not because you cannot memorize other things but you simply see Scripture memorization as being hard or boring. Many of us can quickly memorize song lyrics but find it hard to memorize Bible verses. No one's asking you to memorize the Scripture in a day or two or even in a week, but you can start it bit by bit until you have taken a large chunk of it into your spirit—that's memorization. Biblical meditation begins with committing the Word to memory else there will be nothing to meditate on.

One method to help you memorize Bible verses is through verbal repetition. You will have to take the Word and read it verbally, repeating it over and over. The most important thing here is that you must first have an understanding of what you are taking to heart (*see* Philippians 4:8). From your repetition of the Word, you can begin to talk it in your mind and have it remain in you. No one was born with the Word, but through conscious learning and memorization, they can talk and quote the

Bible like they were born with it. The journey of a thousand mile begins with a bold step. You can start yours today by first reading it, repeating what you have read verbally and doing same in your mind and subsequently meditating on it.

Another important consideration is your motivation to study and meditate on the Word. As Christians, the reality that we cannot please God without faith should motivate us to study the His Word and meditate on it. The Word of God builds faith in us. It is the person of the Word living in us. With faith in us through the Word, we can build a cordial relationship with God and declare His Word with boldness.

God's Word in us is our inheritance from God. Without the Word, there will be nothing for us to show or prove to the world that we are children of God. His Word in us gives us assurances of blessing, protection, wisdom, understanding, and power over sin that causes attacks and sicknesses. These fruits of the Word should give us the utmost motivation that we need to memorize and ultimately meditate on the Word. To learn more, read James 1:25; Joshua 1:8; Psalm 1:2-3, 119:9-11 and 119: 97-102.

To meditate effectively, you must understand the Scripture through Bible study. While meditation is to know God, Bible study is to learn about God. Overall, keep your Holy Bible at the center; depend on the Holy Spirit as your teacher while other things can serve as your aid to knowing God.

To start off with actual memorization, you will need a meditation journal to keep track of your journey through the Scriptures.

For a beginner, 1−3 verses of the Scripture would be fine at once. Don't start by reading long passages; chew it in bits. Ensure that what you previously read settles in you or at least is in the process before going for another verse. Be careful not to overload your brain but try to maintain consistency. That's the key. As you commit the Word into your memory through memorization, grind it with meditation and have it form an integral part of you. While memorization is to the brain; meditation is to the heart or the human spirit with the help of the Holy Spirit. Once you can have the Scripture buried in your spirit, it remains there forever, and you can always declare or call on it with faith when you need it or have it constantly influencing your thoughts and actions. Call the Word in line with your challenges. Like Abraham, be fully persuaded by what you know or believe about God in your spirit.

Chapter 5

3 FORMS OF CHRISTIAN MEDITATION

Biblical meditation can be general, specific or based on the teachings of the Word. General meditation refers to a form of meditation that the result of it can affect your entire being and those around you or in your world. It is a far reaching model of meditation that touches all areas of your life. Example of a general meditation is the closing prayer of the Synagogue Church of All Nations, Nigeria on service days by Prophet TB Joshua.

It goes thus:

"O Holy Spirit, take more of me and give me more of You. Give me more of your love O Holy Spirit. Give me more of Your strength and take more of my weakness. Give me more of Your faithfulness and take more of my unfaithfulness. Give me more of Your humility and take more of my pride. Give me more of Your joy and take more of my unhappiness O Holy Spirit. Give me more of Your purity and take more of my uncleanness. Give me more of Your peace and take more of my worries. Make me a channel of love where there is hatred and a channel of humility where there is pride. Make me a channel of light where there is darkness.

Make me a channel of peace where there is trouble O Holy Spirit."

This is just an example of general meditation. Study the text, and you will realize that it makes a whole lot of sense and can be adopted for a meditation. It's a prayer of exchange of our weakness with the strengths of God. It addresses the primary things that we need to make our walk with God what it should be and also present you as a tool of change and a role model to others. Imagine your life if this becomes a reality for you.

Specific meditation refers to taking a Scripture that addresses a specific need and making such Scripture your meditation to have what it talks about happen in your life. Example, Psalm 1:3 says, "He shall be like a tree planted by the rivers of water, that brings forth its fruit in its season, whose leaf also shall not wither, and whatever he does shall prosper." You can meditate on this and declare that everything you set your hands to do shall prosper as it is promised in this Scripture. Once you are convinced that this is true for you then you don't have any problem. Simply go about your business knowing that God is behind you perfecting the works of your hands to success.

Lastly, a meditation based on teachings of the Word refers to a kind of meditation as a result of a teaching or a testimony of God's grace on someone's life that you listen to and want it to happen in your own life. In church, your minister of God can preach or give a message; all you need to do is to meditate on this message to have it renew your mind and change you to a better person. These messages from them are revelations from God, and you just can't listen to them and go back home without taking them behind you; you must take these messages personally and meditate on them as they come on every service day. Other times, we listen to people's testimony of God's grace in their lives; we can also tap from the grace that comes with those testimonies by meditating on them, and the same miracle would happen in our lives.

CHAPTER 6

WRAP UP: 9 THINGS YOU
SHOULDN'T FORGET ABOUT
MEDITATION

1. Meditation is giving God your
attention

God needs our attention always (*see*
Proverbs 4:20), and through meditation, we
are in tune with Him. Meditation is not a
one-time affair but a constant engagement
of our minds with God. Meditation is a

continuous renewable process of our heart to sync with God's thoughts and plans for our lives.

2. Meditation begins with thinking about the Scripture but goes beyond that

There is nothing wrong with thinking over the Scripture, in fact, that's the starting point of meditation, but you must go beyond that. You must turn the Word over and over in your mind such that if anything happens in your dream, you will ooze the Word and not simply scream and wake up. You should be able to release the Word at any time instead of your fears. Your ability to let out the Word unconsciously instead of your doubts proves the Word has settled and is alive in you. Such feat can only be achieved through meditation.

3. Meditation on the Word is all that we need as Christians

The Word has been given to us as a tool for effective witness. The Word is our life manual. We are not supposed to be running to the Bible when we need the Word. It is meant to live in us. We are supposed to be carriers of the Word. We are not complete without the Word; in it, we live, without it we fall. Fortunately and unfortunately, only through meditation that we can get the Word into our heart and have it richly in us as stated here. *"Let the word of Christ dwell in you richly in all wisdom, teaching and admonishing one another in psalms and hymns and spiritual songs, singing with grace in your hearts to the Lord."* –Colossians 3:16.

4. Regularly reflect and meditate on God: His works and nature

Take a little time and imagine the world before creation. Now, look at where we are today. This is the handiwork of God staring at us. The sky, the sea, the trees, the animals, the hills, and valley, etc. all speak for God anytime we look at them in our heart. These are all wonders of creation. Don't be too busy with life. Once a while, take out quality time, take a walk to some quiet place where you can imagine the wonders of nature. See God in it. Meditate on these beauties of creation, and as you do, you will receive revelations from God.

5. Biblical meditation is different from eastern or new age meditation

The new age meditation meditates on nothing and continuously emphasize on emptying the mind to be filled by some powers. Question: Was anything wrong with the mind before? Absolutely no! This is an extreme and cynical intellectualism which can destroy. Christian meditation, on the other hand, is practically about taking the object of meditation which is the Holy Scripture and exchanging our human thoughts with the thoughts of God to make us mature in the ways of God. Even with that, we are given a check on what kind of thing we should meditate on. It says we should only meditate on whatever is true, honorable, right, pure, lovely, and of good report (*see* Philippians 4:8). This is what we do in Christian meditation. Every other type of meditation for the Christian is evil and should be avoided.

6. Developing the discipline of meditation

Proverbs 4:23 says, *"Keep your heart with all diligence for out of it springs the issues of life."* This Scripture should impact on you the needed discipline to stay your mind on

God's Word. Everything we need in life would come from our hearts, and an empty or corrupted heart can't produce anything meaningful. So rather than allow other things fill up the vacuum of your heart, why not meditate on God's Word? You can go back again and read the benefits of meditation to get some motivation. It isn't something you should miss.

7. Christian meditation is an act of uttering the Scripture with our mouths, considering it thoughtfully and thoroughly; talking and turning it over and over again in our hearts to make it a part of us and declaring same in faith.

8. Create an imagination of what you read to drive in the Word in you

Picture yourself in the Word and what it talks about. See yourself healed, strong and full of life if the Scripture talks about healing.

9. Pray with the meditations of your heart if it leads you into praying

Personalize your meditations to yourself. Praise the Lord and continue living on your meditations. Enjoy your victory in Christ.

CONCLUSION

Acts 19:20 says, *"So the word of the Lord grew mightily and prevailed."* To make the benefits of meditation a constant experience, you must have the Word in you and raise it to a certain level sufficient to produce the faith needed for what you want it to do for you.

Meditation must be a deliberate act to grow your intimacy with God. It goes beyond memorization but taking a hold of the Word in your heart, declaring it in line with your situation and standing in faith to see its manifestation. In every situation, proclaim the Word of God in your spirit. Keep on declaring the Word to renew your heart and faith in God. Remain steadfast in Him.

Visit our website and subscribe to our newsletter:

www.engraftify.com

Printed in Great Britain
by Amazon